The Sky's Not Falling!

Why It's OK to Chill about Global Warming

The Sky's Not Falling!

Why It's OK to Chill about Global Warming

Holly Fretwell

World Ahead Media
Los Angeles, CA

The Sky's Not Falling!
A Kids Ahead Book
Published by World Ahead Media
Los Angeles, CA

Kids Ahead Books are distributed to the trade by:
Midpoint Trade Books
27 West 20th Street, Suite 1102
New York, NY 10011

Kids Ahead Books are available at special discounts for bulk purchases.

World Ahead Publishing also publishes books in electronic formats. For more information call (310) 961-4170 or visit www.worldahead.com.

First Edition
ISBN: 9780976726944
Library of Congress Control Number: 2007932844

Printed in the United States of America

*In hopes that one day all kids
grow up in a healthy environment
in a free and prosperous world.*

The Sky's Not Falling!
Why It's OK to Chill about Global Warming

C O N T E N T S

A Word about (What's In Here) *ix*
Climate Change and Chicken Little *xi*

ONE: Is the Earth *Really* Getting Hotter? *1*
TWO: Global Temperatures Go Up and Down—Naturally! *13*
THREE: What about Warmer Weather Is Wacky? *29*
FOUR: Why Kyoto's a No-Go *41*
FIVE: New Ideas to Rock Your World *59*
SIX: How to Become an "Enviropreneur" *75*

A Word to Parents *117*
Thank Yous *119*
References *121*

A Word about…(What's In Here)

The sky's *not* falling! That is what this book is all about.

But, before we get started on our environmental adventure a word about parentheses. Yes, "(" and ")"!

When you see them anywhere in the book, it means that what's in between is additional information. That information may be clarifying an idea or referring you to a figure or a source. This means that you can actually look up the source where the information came from. The full information about that source can be found at the end of the book in the bibliography. Many of these sources are only several mouse clicks away.

That's an important tool when it comes to making up your own mind!

Climate Change and Chicken Little

There's a famous old story you might remember about a chicken named Chicken Little—a chicken who got scared about something that, in the end, turned out to be nothing but an acorn.

As the story goes, Chicken Little is working in her garden one day when something falls from the sky and lands on her head. Chicken Little, thinking the sky is falling, hurries off to the palace to warn the king.

Chicken Little meets some friends on her way to the palace and tells them that they are in terrible danger. One by one, her friends become as scared as Chicken Little. None of them had actually been hit on the head by a falling piece of sky, but Chicken Little was scared, so they felt scared too.

When Chicken Little and her friends finally arrive at the palace, the wise king listens to their warning. He smiles after Chicken Little finishes telling her story, reaches out his hand, and gently takes a tiny acorn out of the feathers on Chicken Little's head. He reminds the friends that only rain falls from the sky and they have no reason to fear. It's just an acorn. The sky's *not* falling!

Like all good stories, this one has a moral—*we need to check out the facts before getting scared about things*. If Chicken Little had taken the time to look for herself, she would have found the acorn and realized that the sky was not falling. And Chicken Little's friends also learned an important lesson: *Don't believe everything you're told*.

You have probably heard that global warming is a big issue for the world. Some people think we, like Chicken Little, should panic about it. They argue our planet is in danger and we must find a way to save it before it's too late. They believe the earth is warming because of human actions, and that humans like you and me should be forced to stop those actions. Like Chicken Little, they tell their story to anyone who will listen.

You may have heard that burning fossil fuels, such as coal, oil, and gas, will pollute the air until it brings us to the end of humankind. You may have heard that glaciers are melting and mammals, fish, and birds are dying. You may have heard that we might see more hurricanes, big storms, and drought. Nearly every heat wave, hail storm, or weather disturbance is blamed on global warming. So many people now believe these claims that it can be uncomfortable to question them.

Are these people right? Is global warming *really* happening? If it is, did we cause it? More importantly, is global warming a small problem like the acorn in the story, or is it a huge global crisis? Let's look at the facts for ourselves and figure out what's really going on.

Is the Earth
Really Getting Hotter?

To answer our questions about global warming, we need to look first to science and what science tells us about the world and its climate.

What is science? Science is a way of learning. Science gives us a process for finding truth and separating fact from fiction. Science gives us the ability to predict.

But good science depends on good information. Have you ever heard someone say "garbage in, garbage out"? That means if we study untrue information, the things we learn from that information might not be true. The information a scientist uses when doing research must be true. Otherwise, we can't trust the information learned from that research.

While science gives us the best knowledge we have about the natural world, our knowledge constantly changes as scientists study and learn new things. Amazing inventions like the computer and electricity help us gather better information—and more of it.

For example, until six hundred years ago scientists thought that the earth was the center of the universe and that all the planets orbited around it. Further research and new inventions like the telescope enabled scientists to learn that this theory was wrong. We now know that the planets revolve around the sun, not the earth.

What does all of this mean when we talk about global warming? Well, when studying science, we have to remember that what we discover later might disprove what we believe now. And when people are stubborn in their beliefs—like those who thought the earth was the center of the universe—it's difficult to convince them that they're wrong, even when new information appears. Some people believe that humans are causing our planet to warm up, and they can sometimes be very stubborn about their beliefs. But we need to do more studying about our climate before we conclude that this is the case.

The Climate Roller Coaster

Weather is the outdoor conditions that surround us like rain, sun, and wind. You might or might not wear a coat, depending upon the weather (and your mother). We usually consider day-to-day temperature changes as weather and the weather over many years or in different regions as *climate*.

Remember the discovery that the earth revolves around the sun? The earth is part of a vast solar system, and what happens here on Earth depends partly on what happens on the sun. The climate of the earth has cooled and warmed many times since its beginning 4.6 billion years ago. It's a lot like in the movie *Ice Age* and its sequel *The Meltdown*. The earth has had many ice ages and many meltdowns. An ice age happens when huge ice sheets called glaciers cover large areas of the earth.

Glaciers are formed by layers of snow that build up over the years. They grow and expand when the climate cools. They also move like a river, but very, very slowly. Glaciers melt and shrink when it warms. Sometimes they even melt away.

The earth has gone through many ice

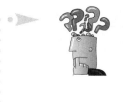

Fun Fact:
Even in the time of dinosaurs, over 100 million years ago, the earth's temperature is believed to have varied.

Fun Fact:
It is known that during the last ice age glaciers expanded into the Midwestern United States.

ages, followed by periods of warming. These periods can last as long as tens to hundreds of thousands of years—longer than humans have lived on Earth (see Figure 1).

The last cooling period ended about ten thousand years ago. Many glaciers have been slowly melting ever since.

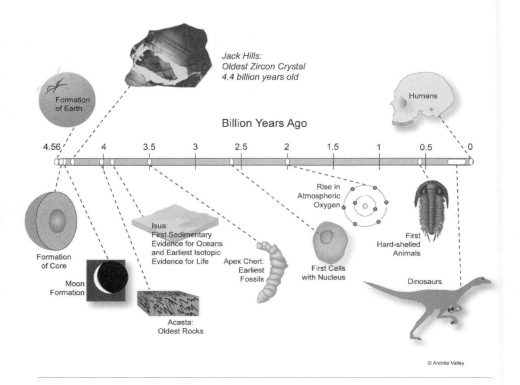

Figure 1: A diagram illustrating major events in earth history. Note that the period of time humans have lived on the earth is much shorter than one warming and cooling cycle. *Timeline courtesy of Andrée Valley, University of Wisconsin.*

4

Figure 2 shows how the earth has warmed and cooled over time. These measurements come from Antarctica. The figure shows the temperature in Antarctica from 650,000 years ago to the present. The present is on the far right at zero years.

As you can see, the climate is in constant change and has been warmer in the past than it is today.

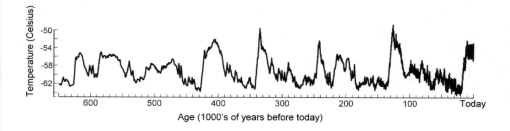

Figure 2: Estimated temperature in Antarctica over the last 650,000 years as derived from polar ice cores. *Figure courtesy of Climate and Environmental Physics, University of Bern, Switzerland.*

Figure 3: A look at air bubbles in polar
ice sheets helps scientists estimate climate
trends from the past. *Photo courtesy of
AP Images/Datsumi Kasahara*

How do we know temperatures from so long ago? Scientists can determine them by drilling deep into the Antarctic ice sheet and removing what is called an ice core.

This ice is hundreds of thousands of years old. As snow falls and freezes year after year, air bubbles get trapped between the layers of snow. The ice cores that scientists remove (see Figure 3) are nearly ten thousand feet long (almost two miles) and contain bubbles of air from up to 650,000 years ago. By studying the air bubbles, scientists can learn about temperatures from the past (Stocker 2007, 13).

The ice cores show that the earth's climate has changed over time, with periods of cooling and warming.

So what does that mean for the future? Should we expect disasters to occur as a result of warming global temperatures?

Now, predicting the future climate is a difficult business. Think of the times the weather forecaster on TV told you it would be sunny for your soccer game but it rained instead. Even with the powerful computers that scientists have today, it is not possible to determine perfectly the many complicated factors that affect the earth's climate.

Remember "garbage in, garbage out"?

Fun Fact:
We only monitor about 10 percent of the globe's glaciers—half are growing, half shrinking!

Fun Fact:
If you had 46 Oreo cookies to signify Earth's age, one for every 100 million years, human life on Earth would be one small crumb.

Fun Fact:
A computer will unquestion-ably use the data it's given. If a person programs into a computer that blue and yel-low make orange and then tells the computer to paint an orange tiger, the comput-er will paint a green tiger. The computer doesn't know any better!

Fun Fact:
The medieval period is also known as the Middle Ages.

Computer models, no matter how advanced, are only as good as the information put into them. If the information is wrong, or if scientists try to measure the wrong thing, the computer model will give a wrong answer. If we don't know what is affecting the earth's climate or how it is being affected, we cannot program the computer to provide accurate predictions.

Although computer models aren't per-fect, they are an important tool for scientists trying to make sense of the many things that can change our climate. And many of today's most advanced computer models predict a warmer future for our planet.

That makes sense. As we've seen, the earth has cooled and warmed in the past, and an ice age ended not too long ago. The amount of warming that has taken place over the last 150 years matches the amount of warming we've seen throughout history whenever the earth is between ice ages—like it is right now. In fact, the amount of warming happening today is close to the natural warming that we know happened between 1905 and 1940. We also know natural warming happened during other periods in the last one thousand years, like a time scientists call the Medieval Warming Period that came between the years

800 and 1300 (Carter et. al. 2006, 173).

Of course, a warming Earth means a changing Earth. But our ability to measure the change has changed, too. Just because you can measure something, though, doesn't mean that the answer you get from those measurements is going to be right. We still have so much more to learn about our climate.

For example, evidence shows that the sea ice in the Arctic has been melting and shrinking (Foley 2005). In Antarctica, however, some areas of sea ice have been expanding (Vaughan 2005). How can the ice shrink in the Arctic while the ice in Antarctica grows? Different places in the world have different temperatures and different levels of moisture.

As we move into the meltdown phase of the last ice age, different places are affected in different ways. In addition, we continue to change the way we measure things as science provides us with more accurate tools.

The truth is that no one, not even the best scientists, knows why some places are becoming warmer and others cooler. We know the temperature around the equator is warmer than around the North and South Poles and that some places have more rain and snow than others. As a result, while some areas see ice decreasing, other areas see it increasing.

While the average global climate does appear to be warming based on the evidence we have now, *we don't know enough to make a good prediction of the future climate of the world.* There are too many factors involved that even the smartest scientists are uncertain about.

If you don't know what is influencing change and how, you can't program your computer to factor it in. What we *do* know is that climate is always changing and that today's global temperature appears to follow the historic patterns of years past—at least the 650,000 that we have observed. That is a very long time. Humans have been on Earth only a short part of that; about 50,000 years.

So what about our effect on the climate? Are we able to tell if the warming that is occurring is caused by people?

Keep reading and find out.

Global Temperatures Go Up and Down– Naturally!

CHAPTER TWO

As we've seen, the last ice age ended ten thousand years ago, and today we are in a warming period. The *reason for* that warming, however, is what everyone is arguing about. Even though the earth's climate has warmed and cooled throughout time, some people blame the bulk of climate change on humans. But is this really true?

In order to determine this, we must first consider something called the atmosphere.

What's In the Air?

The atmosphere is the air that surrounds the

earth and reaches into space. Like a blanket, the atmosphere covers the planet, keeping it warm and safe.

The atmosphere is made up of lots of different gases. The most plentiful is nitrogen, making up nearly 80 percent. Nitrogen is essential for life. It helps plants grow.

Oxygen is the next most plentiful gas, making up about 20 percent of the atmosphere. All living creatures need oxygen to breath. Oxygen also helps them create energy from food.

Greenhouse gases, including carbon dioxide, are another important atmospheric gas. Greenhouse gases make up less than one percent of the atmosphere, but it's an important one percent. They help trap heat close to the earth, like a greenhouse traps heat in a room.

You've probably seen a greenhouse, those small buildings with clear walls that allow sunlight in. Once in, the sunlight warms the plants and soil inside and the clear walls help keep the heat from escaping.

Likewise, greenhouse gases allow light to enter the atmosphere and warm the surface of the earth. As the heat from the earth bounces back into space, greenhouse gases bounce some of the heat back to the earth, or carry it down as moisture, contributing to its warmth.

Fun Fact:
The earth has warmed about 1 degree Fahrenheit in the last 100 years.

14

Without greenhouse gases the earth would be a very cold place to live…if humans and animals could live here at all!

Water vapor is the most common greenhouse gas, which makes up 95 percent of all greenhouse gases. It comes from water evaporating from the surface of oceans, lakes, rivers, and ponds, and even from puddles and dog bowls! In the process, water changes from a liquid to a gas.

Methane is also a greenhouse gas. Methane is released into the air when organic material, like that found in wetlands and swamps, decays and when human waste products, like those found in landfills, dumps, or sewage treatment plants, decompose.

Methane is the main component of natural gas. Methane also comes from livestock and other animal emissions. Yes, poops, belches, farts, and even breathing!

Carbon dioxide is the last major greenhouse gas. Carbon dioxide is made up of carbon and oxygen.

Most living things produce carbon dioxide. Plants absorb carbon dioxide and use it to produce energy and oxygen. Without it, there would be no plant life or oxygen and, therefore, no life on Earth.

Carbon dioxide has a natural cycle. It is

Fun Fact:
Without greenhouse gases the earth would be more like the moon with an average temperature around 0 degrees Fahrenheit. We are fortunate to live with average temperatures closer to 60 degrees Fahrenheit.

Fun Fact:
If methane can be trapped, as it often is at newer landfill sites, it can be used for fuel to provide energy. Many homes are heated with methane from the neighborhood landfill.

Fun Fact:
In New Zealand, belches, farts, and other gaseous emissions from cattle and sheep are a greater source of greenhouse gas than cars.

Fun Fact:
If the gaseous emissions from one adult cow could be collected for a year, it would provide enough energy to fuel a car for more than 600 miles. (Waghorn and Woodward 2003).

released into the atmosphere whenever humans and animals breathe, when forests catch fire, when volcanoes erupt, and when humans burn things, like trees, coal, and gas. These are called "carbon flows" because they flow into the atmosphere.

Plants take the carbon dioxide from the air and hold it like a sponge holds water. Oceans also hold carbon dioxide.

So does the soil. These are called "carbon sinks." Sinks hold carbon out of the atmosphere.

The amount of carbon around the globe is fixed. What changes is the amount held in sinks and the amount that is released by flows.

Figure 4 shows the flows and sinks in billion metric tons. The atmosphere, vegetation and soils, and the surface of the ocean are considered "active" flows because carbon dioxide enters and exits from them daily. Deep ocean layers and deposits in rocks are "inactive" flows because the amount stored changes little over time.

Humans have changed an inactive flow,

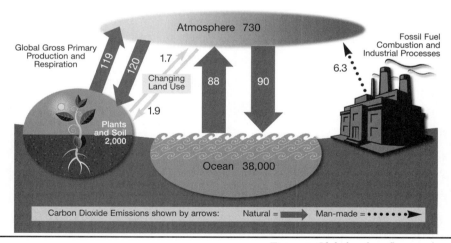

Figure 4: Global carbon flows and sinks. *Based on diagram originally attributed to the Intergovernmental Panel on Climate Change,* Climate Change 2001: The Scientific Basis *(UK, 2001).*

17

carbon stored in fossils, to an active flow by producing and burning fossil fuels (Scarborough 2007, 5).

Concern over CO_2

Many people blame an increase in carbon dioxide, particularly that released by humans from these previously inactive flows, for global warming. They argue that the additional flow of carbon dioxide has overwhelmed the sinks, keeping more carbon dioxide in the atmosphere and thereby warming the earth.

But is this true?

While human-released carbon dioxide has increased, it is not clear that it contributes to global warming. First, it does not appear that the sinks have been overwhelmed by human emissions. Research shows that they absorb at least half of the human-released carbon dioxide. Second, as figure 4 on the previous page demonstrates, the human-released carbon dioxide is a very small portion of the overall cycle.

Fun Fact:
Fuels, such as coal, oil, and gas, are called "fossil fuels" because they come from the fossilized bodies of ancient, prehistoric plants and animals.

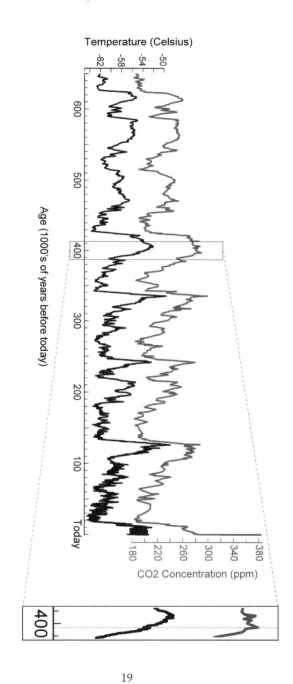

Figure 5: The temperature graph from figure 2 overlayed with a graph illustrating the estimated carbon dioxide levels in Antarctica over the same 650,000 year period. Because the lines of the graphs seem to move together, many people believe that it proves that carbon dioxide causes global warming. However, a closer look at the evidence shows that temperatures peak hundreds or even thousands of years before carbon dioxide levels peak. *Figure courtesy of Climate and Environmental Physics, University of Bern, Switzerland.*

Furthermore, scientists aren't sure if increases in carbon dioxide—human caused or otherwise—are responsible for warmer global temperatures.

Another Side of the Story

It's true that carbon dioxide levels seem to rise and fall in the same way that global temperatures do. Look at Figure 5 from the last page. The black line is the same as the earlier diagram showing the temperature changes estimated from the Antarctic ice sheet.

The temperature is shown on the left scale. The grey line is the estimated level of carbon dioxide in the atmosphere and is shown on the right scale. The data is calculated using the air bubbles from the same polar ice core we talked about earlier.

You can see that the two lines move together. During ice ages, when the temperature is cold, carbon dioxide levels stay low and show up near the bottom of the graph.

During warmer periods, between ice ages, both lines move up like mountains. In other words, in the past, temperatures have been warmer when carbon dioxide levels are higher.

Does this mean that changes in carbon dioxide levels *cause a change in the global tem-*

Fun Fact:
In medieval times, around the year 1000, people called the Vikings inhabited Greenland, a country that is now largely covered in ice. They farmed in soil that is now permanently frozen called permafrost.

perature? Not necessarily, though many people believe this to be true. It's like the question of which came first, the chicken or the egg.

A closer look at the evidence behind the diagram shows that temperatures rise hundreds or even thousands of years before carbon dioxide levels rise. The temperature often peaks and begins to fall before carbon dioxide levels fall (Fischer et al. 1999).

This answers the question of which came first: temperatures changed first. This does not agree with the story some people tell. If the temperature changed *before* the carbon dioxide levels rose, carbon dioxide levels are probably not the cause of the temperature change.

This contradicts the assumption that increased carbon dioxide will cause increased temperature. It contradicts the assumption used in most climate models that predict future temperatures.

In fact, the warming trend may not be related to human activity at all. How do we know? For one thing, scientists believe that about one thousand years ago during a time called the Medieval Warming Period, temperatures were at least as warm as they are today. One thousand years ago, humans did not have cars or factories. No one had invented them yet. So we weren't burning fossil fuels to run factories one thousand years ago, and we weren't putting very much carbon dioxide into the atmosphere.

The only possible global warming and cooling back then would have been natural—not manmade.

After about three hundred years of warmer temperatures in the Medieval Warming Period, the temperature dropped, bringing a time of much colder temperatures called the Little Ice Age.

This all makes it highly unlikely that the current warming trends are a result of human activity. As we saw in Chapter One, we are in the middle of a cycle of warming and cooling that has been going on for a very long time.

There are also other reasons to think that human activity isn't responsible for the warming trends. From the early 1900s to about 1940, a time when your grandparents may have been alive, temperatures rose even though carbon dioxide emissions were low. In the following years, 1940–1975, the temperature increase was slower even though carbon dioxide emissions were greater—a result of industrial development.

Again, the facts don't fit the theory that rising human carbon dioxide emissions cause warmer global temperatures.

And another thing, Earth isn't the only planet warming up. The climate on Mars has been warming too. As a result, the polar ice cap on Mars is shrinking. Human carbon dioxide emissions do not affect the atmosphere of Mars. And, as far as we know, Martians have not been driving around in SUVs burning fossil fuels.

The warming on Mars is like the warming we're seeing on Earth. If it's happening on Mars, where there are no humans, how can we be sure that humans cause global warming on Earth?

The answer is that we can't.

We've seen three big reasons why humans cannot have caused global warming all by themselves:

1. Warming happened on Earth long before humans and long before humans had modern technology;
2. The earth warmed more slowly between 1940 and 1975, when there were higher carbon dioxide emissions, than it did between 1900 and 1940, when there were lower carbon dioxide emissions;
3. Warming is occurring on Mars, where humans don't live at all.

These all suggest humans are not to blame for the warming trends. What, then, *does* cause global warming?

There are many natural reasons that the earth has cooled and warmed over its many years of existence. Cosmic rays are one reason. Scientists have known for years that the earth is constantly bombarded with cosmic rays. Cosmic rays are small particles, like dust, that enter the earth's atmosphere from space. While sending heat energy they also meet with water vapor to form clouds. Low clouds block some of the sun's rays and help cool the earth.

Scientists have found a direct relationship between cosmic rays and the earth's temperature. Over the last one hundred years they have found fewer cosmic rays and fewer clouds. As a result, the sun's energy has grown more intense.

But there are many other factors besides cosmic rays that impact the earth's climate.

Because all these factors interact with each other in ways we don't fully understand, it is difficult to predict the future climate of the world.

- The sun is like a huge explosion. It sends heat energy to the earth and other planets. The amount of heat

Fun Fact:
Cosmic rays are particles from outer space that bombard the earth. They're everywhere!

24

energy it sends changes over time.

- Particles floating in the air can reflect the sun's rays and increase cloud cover. Both the particles and cloud cover can affect global temperature.

- The earth's orbit affects global temperatures. The earth does not rotate around the sun in a continuous circular pattern; rather, its path goes from nearly circular to oval. Sometimes the earth is farther away from the sun than at other times.

- The tilt of the earth affects climate. The North and South Poles are not always the same distance from the sun. This is what brings different climates in summer and winter, and why seasons in the northern half of the earth are opposite those in the southern. Like a top it even wobbles, which also affects Earth's temperature.

- The movements of continents, the rise and fall of ocean depths, and earthquakes have all been shown to influence the earth's climate.

- The formation of mountains and rising land levels seem to have an effect on global temperature.

- Changing ocean currents and changing

air currents influence the climate.
- Gases in the earth's atmosphere may affect its cooling and warming. Remember, without greenhouse gases we would be very cold.

As you can see, there is a long list of natural reasons for global warming. If human actions do have an effect on global warming, it is only one of many.

What about Warmer Weather Is Wacky?

CHAPTER THREE

One of the main beliefs that fuels all the concern about global warming is that it is bad for humans and animals. But is this true? Will increasing global temperatures and carbon dioxide levels have dreadful consequences for the earth's population?

Before we run off in a tizzy like Chicken Little, let's examine this question.

The Good Side of Carbon Dioxide
Carbon dioxide is necessary for life. Humans and animals exhale it when they breathe and plants absorb it and use it to grow. More car-

bon dioxide in the air helps plants grow faster and produce more fruit. Commercial growers even add carbon dioxide to the air in their greenhouses to encourage faster growth and bigger plants.

Additional carbon dioxide in the air also helps plants store more water. That means plants don't need as much water to grow, which means they can grow better in dry places. Better plant growth makes it easier to grow food. This means food could become more plentiful and starvation and famine less likely. This would be a good thing for people and animals.

So more carbon dioxide could actually help feed more people. What about warmer weather? Could worldwide warmer temperatures actually help people? Let's look at some possible results of warmer weather and see.

The Benefits of a Warmer Earth

What is the best temperature? For a lot of people, the answer might be whatever temperature they're used to.

You might prefer hot days when you can play on the beach and lie in the grass. Or maybe you like rainy days when you can curl up with a good book like *The Cat in the Hat.* Possibly snowy days riding a snowboard are more your style.

Whatever your favorite weather, we all have different preferences.

Of course, when the climate changes, there is a lot more at stake than personal preference. Climate changes affect rainfall, plant life, and habitat. Climate changes can also affect how we live, what we wear, and what we do for a living. Many of us live in places where there are four distinct seasons—spring, summer, fall, and winter. We're used to adapting as the seasons change. We wear our sweaters in October and bathing suits in July.

While it might require larger adaptations, there is no reason we cannot do the same when it comes to global warming. Human beings are amazingly flexible!

Many climate models predict that most of the warming will take place on winter nights. They also predict that the regions around the North and South Poles will warm more than the regions around the equator. In the United States, this means warmer temperatures, especially up north. Minnesota and New York are likely to warm more than Florida and Texas. In other words, global warming could make areas with harsh weather more pleasant while still keeping pleasant areas nice.

Aside from making us more comfortable, these changes could result in energy savings. Because people in formerly cold areas will not need to run the heat as often, energy use could decrease. Fewer mornings will require shoveling snow and scraping ice, and the roads will not be treacherous as often, resulting in fewer weather-related deaths (Davis et.al. 2003).

Shorter winters and warmer nights will also mean a longer harvest season, giving farmers more time to grow their crops. This, plus the carbon dioxide–caused boost in plant growth that we've already discussed, means that global warming could result in better food growth per acre.

More food per acre means we could devote less land to farming and use more land for wildlife habitats and forest preservation.

Stormy Weather
We've all seen storms ravage regions and destroy communities. Hurricane Katrina in 2005 was a frightening reminder of the immense power of nature. Some people say these storms are becoming more devastating because of global warming and will only get worse as the warming increases.

It may be true that more people are affected by large storms today than were affected in the past. More homes and business are destroyed, more livelihoods are taken away. But that's partly because more people live in the path of such storms, not that the storms themselves have become larger or more powerful due to global warming! As a result, the costs of storm damage have increased too.

In the United States more people today live along the coastline than ever before. We know more storms hit the coast than inland regions. The evidence is *not* clear that global warming is causing more storms. It *is* clear that more people live in areas where storms hit. Not only that, but we know about more storms than we used to because we have satellite technology that lets us see many more storms than we knew existed before.

Rising Sea Levels

Some global warming theories have predicted that if the storms don't devastate coastal communities, rising sea levels will. Examining ice sheets worldwide helps scientists predict possible changes in sea level. Melting glaciers would mean more water in the oceans and the possibility of sea level rising. Increasing quantities of ice would mean more water stored as ice, which means sea level falling.

In truth, we need to look at sea level

changes from several points of view. It is often the land that is rising or sinking, not the sea. Remember, the earth is in constant change. Land in Holland, for example, has been sinking for years. So has land in New Orleans and the entire Gulf Coast.

Second, there is a difference between glaciers of the last ice age, which were huge land-based glaciers, and the sea ice of today. As the land-based glaciers melted, the sea level rose steadily as it has done for eight thousand years. That rate of increase has slowed in the last one hundred years. Most of the two largest ice sheets today, in Antarctica and Greenland, flow over the ocean and are already below sea level. If they were to melt, sea level would not rise very much.

Contrary to what most people think, when ice melts its size decreases. This is because water expands when it freezes; therefore, the ice occupies more space than the water it contains. That is why ice floats. It is also why your kitchen pipes will break if they freeze. (Ask your dad!) Most of the Arctic ice is already in the water; its melting will cause only a small change in sea level.

In addition, the ice mass of both Greenland and Antarctica is increasing (Vaughan 2005, Johannessen et al. 2005). It is very important to understand that glaciers are as much a function of snowfall as they are of temperature. For example, the glaciers on Mt. Kilimanjaro are getting smaller, yet the temperature is never above freezing. The ice evaporates but there is no moisture to replace the loss.

One of the worst case scenarios for sea level is that it could increase by close to two feet over the next one hundred years (IPCC 2007, 13). This conclusion is based on the most pessimistic temperature models.

Now two feet is not a lot. Sea level changes all the time. In fact, though sea level has been rising, it is rising more slowly than it has in the past. It is more likely that changes in sea level will follow the recent slowing trend of a six-inch rise over the last one hundred years or rise even less (Holgate 2007).

Whatever the case, humans have shown themselves capable of adapting to much more drastic changes, so even the worst case shouldn't pose a tragic problem.

In past ice ages, the sea level has changed a lot. About twenty thousand years ago, the sea level was eighty-two feet lower than it is today!

History also shows periods when it was more than one thousand feet higher than today (Lambeck and Chappell 2001). Such large changes in sea levels happen over tens to hundreds of thousands or even millions of years.

Remember, humans have been on Earth only about fifty thousand years, with the industrial age only a few hundred years old. It is unlikely that Los Angeles or New York City will be drowning under water any time soon—and less likely that humans would be responsible for it.

Do It for the Animals!

You probably love animals, and it's scary to hear about how melting glaciers and ice sheets might be causing polar bears to drown and penguins to die. Polar bears live in the Arctic. They float on sea ice and dive off to catch their food. It has been argued that sea ice in the Arctic has been declining. This may mean that polar bears have less space in which to live.

Studies on world polar bear populations, however, show that while the numbers of some polar bear populations are declining, other populations are stable and some are even growing (IUCN/SSC, 2005). Truth be told, we don't know how many polar bears live in most regions. Polar bears live in places that are too cold for humans, so it's hard to know for sure if total polar bear numbers are rising or falling,

Fun Fact:
Polar bears don't live in the Antarctic. The penguins and seals that live there should like that just fine, too!

since we can't be there to see it for ourselves. And indeed, they have survived warming in the past and will likely survive warming today.

In Antarctica, at the opposite end of the earth, total sea ice is growing, and the penguins and seals that live there should like that just fine (Vaughan 2005).

One Fish, Two Fish, More Fish, Few Fish?

As the earth warms, the ocean surface will probably warm, too. Does warmer ocean water mean more or fewer fish? One theory says that as water warms there will be fewer fish because warmer water means less dissolved oxygen for the fish to breathe. Dissolved oxygen is the amount of oxygen found in water.

Fun Fact:
Just like you and I need oxygen, or air, to breathe, so do fish.

On the other hand, scientists have found warmer waters where fish have grown faster and more plentiful. Just like some plants grow better in warmer temperatures, fish can, too. Increased ocean temperatures might actually be good for fish (Thresher et al. 2007).

So does a warmer climate and warmer water mean more or fewer fish? The answer is that we really don't know. The changes could be positive or negative.

We need to know more, but it is important to consider both possibilities before deciding what, if anything, people should do about the fish population.

Without better knowledge about how the natural world will respond to warmer temperatures, and with so many different personal preferences among humans, it's difficult to determine whether warming is good or bad.

What we need to understand is that change occurs all the time and nature has built-in mechanisms for adapting to these changes. However, the lack of good information and many uncertainties have not stopped people from making scary predictions.

With these predictions have come many recommendations that would affect the way we live. Let's think about some of those recommendations.

Why Kyoto's
a No-Go

CHAPTER FOUR

You've probably heard the saying "better safe than sorry." When it comes to the planet's current warming trend, this is the attitude that many people are adopting.

They say that even though the science behind global warming is uncertain, and even though it is not clear that the current warming trend is bad, we should do something in case the consequences are worse than we think. Are they right?

The answer is yes and no.

Some things are just plain good to do, no matter what the truth is about global warming. For instance, adopting energy-saving habits, such as carpooling or turning off lights when they are not in use can be a good thing. Why waste nature's gifts?

Solutions developed and sold by individuals and private companies can also be good things to do. One of the main reasons for this is that they must compete in the marketplace to be a success. That means people like you and me are making decisions to exchange our hard-earned cash for the solution.

That's quite a vote of confidence! We'll look at these types of solutions in more depth in Chapter Five.

Other solutions, such as those provided by government, can sometimes cause more problems than they solve.

They often impose unnecessary restrictions and costs on people and result in unintended consequences. This is because the people who develop the government solutions don't pay their full cost—other people do.

Outlawing certain types of cars, taxing fuels so that they're more expensive to buy, and supporting questionable alternative energies are all examples of how government tries to solve things.

We'll look at each of these in more depth as we go through this chapter.

Road Regs

Think about how you might add to a collection—for example, a collection of baseball cards. If cards cost $1 a piece and you have $5, you can buy five cards. If the price falls to two cards for $1, you can now buy ten cards. You can get more for your money, and as a result, you will probably buy more cards. The same is true for gasoline and the number of miles a person drives.

A 1975 law requiring improved auto efficiency in the United States is a case in point. The law required auto makers to build cars that could drive at least 27.5 miles on one gallon of gas. The goal was to decrease the amount of gas we use. Sounds reasonable doesn't it? If a person can go the same number of miles with less gas, they will use less gas, right? Not exactly.

The regulation made driving cheaper. As a result, people drove more miles because they could afford to do so. Similar to the collection of baseball cards, when driving is cheaper, people drive more.

This unintended consequence also happens for other items that have become more energy efficient and, therefore, cheaper to use, including airplane travel, washing clothes, and electricity use in general. In every case, people

43

tend to buy more of something when it becomes cheaper.

Another unintended consequence of the law was that it made cars less safe. In order to meet the mileage requirements, auto makers built smaller, lighter cars.

Smaller, lighter cars are at risk of greater damage in a crash. Greater damage in a crash means greater risk of death or injury. The end result has been *more deaths* from auto accidents (Coon, 2001).

In addition, the law sent the family station wagon and other large cars the way of the dodo bird, which is now extinct! These cars were too large and heavy to meet the fuel efficiency requirements.

To replace the station wagon, families and soccer moms found the newest vehicles with third row seats; the sports utility vehicle or SUV.

Considered a "truck," SUVs do not have to meet the same strict regulation (Coon, 2001). So began the American love affair with the SUV which often burns more gas per mile driven than the old station wagon. Again, the end result was to use *more,* not less, gas.

In light of global warming and the assumption by many that carbon dioxide is causing it, it has been proposed to increase vehicle efficiency standards even further. Will this really reduce emissions? Think about it!

So, one way governments seek to solve environmental problems is by restricting what sellers can sell and, therefore, what buyers can buy. As we have seen, such restrictions can backfire. Another way governments seek to solve environmental problems is by taxing things.

The Tax Man

Imagine if there was a TV tax and you had to pay $5 per hour just to watch. Would you watch more or less TV? Most of us would watch less.

Likewise, governments can change what we purchase by increasing an item's cost through taxation. One example would be raising taxes on fossil fuels, like gasoline. Just like the TV tax, taxing gas discourages people from using as much of it, thereby reducing carbon dioxide emissions. Sounds great, right?

But there's more to it than that. Your parents already pay plenty of taxes on gas, which is money they can't spend on other things like your education, a vacation, housing, food, or even games and toys. Increasing these taxes would make it harder to pay for other needs that we have.

A higher price for gas and other fossil

fuels would make it more expensive to go places and more expensive to make things. Imagine that you have a lawn mowing service. You mow your neighbor's lawn for $8 a week. You have to buy one gallon of gas each week to mow the lawn. When gas is $3 per gallon you can save $5 a week to buy a new game or something you want.

Now, imagine a new gas tax. Gas is now going to cost you $5 per gallon. Would you still be willing to mow the neighbor's lawn? At $8 per week you might not, because you'll only earn $3 for the time you're spending. In order to make it worth your effort, you'll need to ask your neighbor to pay more. When the costs of production increase (like the cost of gas for the mower) the price of the final product (the mowed lawn) usually increases as well.

In the same way, a tax that increases the price of energy would result in higher prices for many other items. Because the fuel used to make things would cost more, nearly *everything* would cost more. Store prices would also go up reflecting higher shipping costs.

Higher taxes on gas and other fossil fuels would likely reduce the amount of fuel we use, which would in turn reduce carbon dioxide emissions. We don't, however, really know the benefits from less carbon dioxide in the air.

We do know there are unintended consequences from the tax—more expensive heating and transportation and higher prices for the things we buy.

The people most hurt by a fuel tax are those people who have the least amount of money to spend.

Some would find other ways to get by, like burning wood in their fireplace to heat their house instead of using fossil fuels, ways that could easily lead to more pollution. People who can barely afford to buy the necessities they need to live will now have to spend more on those necessities.

Growing Energy

So, government rules that attempt to restrict or discourage certain actions can have high costs and unintended consequences.

What about government actions that instead try to *encourage* certain behavior?

Have you ever offered to help a friend pay for a movie or lunch just so that they'll go with you? Sometimes the government does just that to encourage people to act in a certain way. A good example is the way they're trying to encourage the use of alternative fuels, for instance, instead of gasoline.

One energy source that government has

targeted in this way can actually be grown on the farm. Cool, huh? It is called biofuel and is made from biomass like corn, switch grass, and sugar cane.

The U.S. government has set a goal to replace some of our gasoline use with biofuels, mostly ethanol. Ethanol is a biofuel produced with corn or other crops. To encourage the use of ethanol, the government is paying corn farmers and ethanol producers to keep the price lower than it would otherwise be. Corn farmers and ethanol producers, of course, really like this and have increased their production as a result.

While this sounds incredibly cool, we need to ask if ethanol is the energy source we should be investing in. Government actions are funded, not by government workers, but by all taxpayers. And the intention of funding ethanol production is to benefit society. But there are costs to society as well.

Making ethanol requires energy and resources. Sometimes we expend more money and resources than we get back in energy! And burning ethanol often produces more carbon dioxide than burning fossil fuels. Let's look closely at these costs and the unintended consequences of expanding ethanol use.

• The production of ethanol from corn

Fun Fact:
Biomass is material from living or recently living things, like grass, crops, trees, or even animal poop.

requires growing corn.

- Corn production requires lots of land—land that we could use for growing other crops, building houses, or preserving wildlife.
- Corn production requires tractors which use fuel. Fuel emits carbon dioxide.
- Fertilizers are often used to produce corn. The manufacturing process of fertilizers requires burning fossil fuels. Fertilizer use increases water pollution from runoff.
- When more corn is used for ethanol, there is less corn available for livestock feed and human consumption. This results in higher corn prices.
- Higher corn prices lead to increased prices for other products made from corn—for instance, the beef, pork, and chicken that comes from corn-fed animals or corn-based foods such as Doritos and tortillas.
- Ethanol is not as efficient at producing energy as fossil fuels. It requires more gallons of ethanol than gas to drive the same distance in a car.
- When the government pays farmers and ethanol makers it cannot use that

Fun Fact:
According to the Department of Energy "Almost all of the arable [farmable] land on Earth would need to be covered with the fastest-growing known energy crops, such as switchgrass, to produce the amount of energy currently consumed from fossil fuels annually." (U.S. DOE 2005 x)

money for other purposes, like education and national security.

- Many developing countries are clearing forest land to grow crops for biofuels like ethanol. The trees removed can no longer absorb carbon dioxide from the air and many are burned sending out the carbon dioxide
they once held.

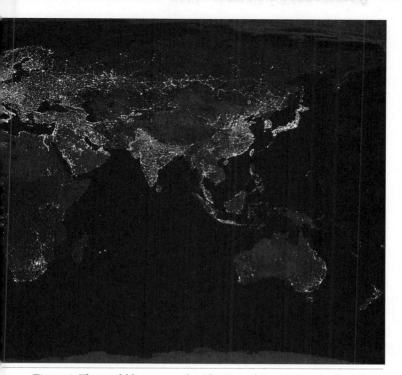

Figure 6: The world lit up at night. The United States is on the far left. You can see for yourself how much more light and energy developed countries use. *Data courtesy Marc Imhoff of NASA GSFC and Christopher Elvidge of NOAA NGDC. Image by Craig Mayhew and Robert Simmon, NASA GSFC.*

So, as you can see, government financing encourages ethanol production without considering the full costs or the unintended consequences. Government workers don't pay the price when such programs fail. Nor do they lose their jobs, like people who make poor decisions in regular jobs often do. What such policies do is make biofuels *appear* cheaper than they really are so people buy more than they otherwise would.

In other words, the government is encouraging biofuel use by using tax money to make it seem like a better deal than it really is. In the case of biofuels, the costs to society may be greater than the benefits.

Before encouraging government financial support we should ask, does government really know what is best for us?

Does government know what technologies will thrive and which will fail? When a company makes a product and sells it in the market, it succeeds or fails based on how well the desires of buyers are met.

When it comes to government, even programs that satisfy few and have large costs are often funded for years—even decades!

Kyoto

Even within the boundaries of just one country, the United States, and even with well-defined goals, government solutions can be costly and have unintended consequences. Unfortunately, despite a dismal track record, people are now suggesting that government solutions be used on a global scale to combat global warming.

In 1997, a number of world leaders met in Kyoto, Japan, to discuss climate-related issues. The result of the meeting is an agreement called the Kyoto Treaty. The treaty requires developed countries, such as the United States, Great Britain, and Japan, to reduce their greenhouse gas emissions below their 1990 levels.

The agreement has been signed by over 160 countries, but not the United States or Australia. This is the most far-reaching regulation-based solution to global warming that has ever been proposed.

The agreement exempts developing countries like China, India, and a number of African nations.

Yet developing nations have faster growth in population and carbon dioxide emissions than developed countries! In fact, China is the world's biggest carbon dioxide emitter. These exemptions still make sense because forcing developing countries to reduce their emissions is like forcing them to remain undeveloped and poor. Developing economically requires the use of energy, usually in the form of fossil fuels.

Historically, economic development has been one of the best things that a country can do to help its people and reduce pollution.

The growth of developing countries, however, depends upon technological advances in developed countries. That's

Fun Fact:
Some people in developing countries now have cell phones even though they never had, or never will have, the telephone wires necessary for a land line.

53

because developing countries can then use the new technology without paying the costs of creating and testing it.

History has shown that developed countries are much better at achieving these advances because of their greater wealth and their better educated populations.

In this way, there is a strong connection between human well-being in developed and developing countries.

When prices in developed countries rise, it is more expensive for developing countries to access the new technology. When prices in developed countries rise, like they would with an energy tax or forced emissions reduction, we spend more money on necessities.

As a result, we have less left over to invest in innovation and to buy from developing countries.

This means slower growth and lower incomes for people in both developed and developing regions! In some regions of the world, this slowdown could literally be the difference between life and death. We need to be very careful before adopting a policy with such serious consequences.

Furthermore, the impact that a reduction of carbon dioxide levels will have on climate change is not yet clear. Most scientists agree that even with the Kyoto Treaty some warming will still occur. Even if carbon dioxide levels stay where they are or are reduced, there is no guarantee it will have any impact on the global temperature (King 2004; Caldeira and Jain 2003).

In a wealthy country like the United States, there are people willing to spend extra money for cleaner energy sources. But in developing countries many people still worry about how to earn enough money just to feed their families. They worry more about eating today than clean air tomorrow. They are only beginning their industrial revolution, which will bring with it development, higher incomes, and higher levels of carbon dioxide emissions.

It is just that type of development that provides fresh drinking water and sanitation. Development also brings electricity and running water, indoor plumbing, and vaccines. It allows people to make a better life for themselves and their families. Development helps dreams take flight.

When people demand that poor countries reduce their fossil fuel use, they are hurting poor people, not helping them.

When the innovation of entrepreneurs in developed countries is blocked by regulations and high costs, people in developing countries, too, must do without those new technologies.

Now, it's true that industrialization can be dirty. The energy it needs to fuel its growth also pollutes. So while building factories and power plants helps increase productivity and wealth, it also increases some types of pollution—at first. In the United States, during the Industrial Revolution, homes were sold using advertisements that showed smokestacks in the background. The smokestacks meant that industry and good jobs were nearby—it was a good thing. Today, we still want good jobs, but we also want to live where flowers bloom and birds sing.

What does all this teach us about dealing with environmental problems like global warming? As people become wealthier they do more to protect and improve the environment because they can afford to. They are willing to pay more for environmental quality, and pollution levels decline.

If we want a cleaner world *we need to make sure people can afford to care* about the environment. The best way to ensure people can afford to care is to encourage economic growth, not restrict it as Kyoto would do. We'll look more at the growth approach to environmental issues in the next chapter.

New Ideas
to Rock Your World

"World resources running out"

**"World braces itself
for energy shortages"**

**"Energy producers struggle
to keep up with demand"**

Does this sound like today's news? Actually, newspapers ran headlines like these over 100 years ago!

Only back then, people were worried about running out of wood, not gas or coal.

They fretted about forests being cut down and predicted that we would run out of wood to use for heating. In fact, in 1905 President Theodore Roosevelt claimed that a timber famine was inevitable.

Wood was not only the main source of heat for millions of people in the United States and worldwide, but it was also used to build homes, fences, railroad tracks, and bridges. Many forests were cleared so farmers could grow crops. The fear of a timber shortage was very real. And yet, one hundred years later, we still have plenty of wood. So what happened?

As wood became less available and more expensive, smart people all over the world started looking for an alternative and found coal. Beginning in the 1900s, coal began to replace wood as a fuel source.

In this chapter we are going to take a closer look at a few recent examples of this amazing ability of people to adapt and innovate. You'll see that markets and human innovation are a great way to solve problems—perhaps even those created by global warming.

More on Wood and Coal

Let's continue our story about wood and coal. As people began switching from wood to coal, that's when things really got exciting. Because

Fun Fact:
There are more acres of forestland in the United States today than there were in 1920.

Fun Fact:
Wood is still the main source of energy for heat in many developing countries.

coal provided more energy at less cost, it brought energy to more people. In the past energy was very expensive. Outside of big cities, many people could not afford to light their homes. There were few electric appliances or conveniences.

That's why the discovery of coal as an energy source was revolutionary! Once there was a cheap, powerful, plentiful source of energy, electrification spread like wildfire. With this powerful new energy source, scientists, engineers, and inventors created more powerful engines, which in turned powered the creation of the greatest economy the world has ever known.

Today, coal is the major energy source in the United States (Shelton 1982, 2). In fact, coal has become such an important source of energy that people are concerned that we might run out of it too! But we haven't, and we won't.

Innovation and technology brought us oil and gas, which quickly replaced coal for some uses. And, of course, we soon found even more exciting ways to use these new sources of energy. No government regulation or restrictions powered the shift from wood to coal, or coal to oil and gas.

It was rising prices coupled with human

creativity. Once the cost of coal approached that of wood, people switched.

The same thing happened with oil and gas as coal became more expensive. Meanwhile, seeing the opportunity to make a profit, people produced more of these new forms of energy, bringing the price down even further. In the process, millions of lives have been improved and enriched.

And the beat goes on! As fossil fuels become more expensive both in dollar and environmental costs, we're starting the shift towards newer and cleaner technologies. And again, the government doesn't need to force or regulate this shift. Once new technologies emerge at competitive prices, consumers make the shift themselves.

Air Conditioning – A Cool Idea

Another example of innovation is air conditioning—that wonderful cool air we take for granted at movie theaters, in our cars, and in our homes. People lived for thousands of years without it, so how did it come to be?

Actually it was invented to solve a specific problem in a specific industry—the printing industry.

Print quality suffers in humidity, so printers needed something to control the temperature and humidity in the air. Recognizing the opportunity, a man named Willis Carrier invented the air conditioner. He soon realized that lots of industries—not to mention homes—would benefit from reliable cooling. So in 1915 he founded the Carrier Air Conditioning Company of America to create different kinds of air conditioners. Soon Carrier had produced air conditioners to cool houses, offices, and even cars.

Genius!

By allowing people to work longer and more productively, the air conditioner has been a major contributor to economic growth ever since. Not only that, it has saved lives!

So, long story short, too much humidity was causing a problem. Confident that solving the problem would be profitable, an innovator created the air conditioner. The result? Not just many lives saved, but millions of lives made better each and every day! That's how markets motivate people to dream up new and improved ideas that make a difference for everyone.

Food Glorious Food

Like the fear of timber famine, over the years many people have feared that the earth would literally run out of food. But again, human ingenuity has come to the rescue! In the United States we can now grow more than twice the amount of wheat on the same plot of land as fifty years ago. The output per acre from vegetable crops has grown even more. And this technology is spreading throughout the world to feed more people using less land and resources.

The market, where buyers and sellers voluntarily exchange items, brought this about.

Seeing a need for new ways to grow and harvest plants and vegetables, innovators came up with tractors, new kinds of seeds, fertilizers, and ways to keep pests away from growing crops. They came up with new ways to harvest and bring fresh food safely to people just like you.

Today scientists are busy unlocking the secrets of plants, fruits, vegetables and soil. We know more now than ever before about smart ways to grow food in even the most unforgiving places.

Sure, just as in the past, these innovative scientists are energized by the desire to make a profit and a better living for themselves and their families.

But guess what? Food scientists are also saving lives and improving health around the world by the work they are doing! This is the beauty of markets—they let you do well by doing good.

Let's Get Healthy

Another example of our ability to triumph over the environment can be seen in the case of malaria. Malaria is a life-threatening disease carried by mosquitoes. It is widespread in much of the developing world and in warm, tropical areas. More than one million people die from malaria every year.

But don't let anyone tell you that malaria is a warm-weather disease that will inevitably spread around the globe as temperatures rise! The fact is that, no matter what the temperature, malaria is both preventable and curable. Malaria was once common in the United States and found as far north as Minnesota—no tropical paradise.

Malaria didn't disappear from our country because the climate eventually cooled, because we wished it away, or because the government ordered it.

It disappeared because smart people did something about it. Malaria disappeared because of innovation in the form of improved pesticides, cleaner water, and higher living standards. It disappeared because doctors learned how to treat it, and because drug companies came up with new products and ways to combat it.

By cleaning up their water supplies and spraying for mosquitoes, developing nations, even in hot places, will also be able to reduce their malaria problems dramatically (Goklany 2005). Creative minds have already shown the way!

So new technologies bring progress. It's innovators, not government, who have provided us with clean water, clean air, and good health care. It's innovators, not government, who have created things like dishwashers, washing machines, dryers, telephones, and automobiles. It's innovation that has given us the leisure time to enjoy Gameboys, Nintendos, movies, and Heelys.

And the world is wealthier and healthier because of it.

Now that we have the leisure time that power-driven conveniences provide us, we have time to think about and care for things like the environment. A subsistence farmer who must work sixteen hours a day to feed his or her family does not. So it's easy to see why a strong economy and the freedom to create are so important.

Some people argue that because a warmer Earth potentially means big problems, that big government must be in control. But as we've seen, it's the market and competition that are truly the source of the big ideas that solve big problems!

Government can help protect our freedom and our rights but it is not very good at providing the items we need and desire.

Innovation and Global Warming

Now that we've seen where new ideas and new products *really* come from, let's consider how markets and innovation will work when it comes to energy and the possibility of humans causing climate change.

As we have seen, many people believe that human emissions of carbon dioxide are the cause of global warming. But even though there are good reasons to doubt this claim, it may not even be worth arguing about. If we just allow the market to work, the same type of clever, creative people who brought us cooler air, more food, and better health, will come up with a better source of energy than fossil fuels.

Of course, there are challenges ahead. Clean renewable energy sources are still far more expensive and a lot less reliable than electricity produced with coal or gas. That's why they aren't used much…yet.

Still, there are several technologies out

Fun Fact:
Anthropogenic is a term used to describe things that are caused by humans rather than other forces of nature.

there that could become major sources of energy in the near future.

Let's look at three of them:

Catch the Wind

Holland brings images of old windmills and wooden shoes. Some of those old windmills are still in use. But like the move from wood to coal, oil and gas in the United States, Holland moved away from wind to fossil fuels. Will

wind power help us move "back to the future?"

One problem with looking to the wind to provide energy is that it's not always windy. When there's no wind, no energy is produced. We need to learn how to store wind energy cheaply. If you depend upon the wind you either need a backup energy source or you have to wait for the wind to kick up again, and that's no way to power a modern economy!

Still, wind is one of the fastest-growing energy sources worldwide, and smaller, more

Fun Fact:
Windmills covering an area the size of Germany would reduce carbon dioxide emissions by 1 billion tons per year.

energy sources worldwide, and smaller, more efficient windmills are coming online all the time. Germany, Spain, the United States, India, and Denmark are just a few of the countries that use wind power. Use of wind energy tripled between 1999 and 2004 (Benitez et al. 2007, 2). If wind power is going to be the energy source of the future, it's innovators who will get us there.

Fun Fact:
Solar panels would have to cover an area the size of New Jersey to reduce carbon dioxide emissions by 1 billion tons per year.

Harnessing the Sun

The sun is the earth's natural energy source. Every day the sun bombards us with more than nine thousand times the amount of energy humans use each day. But just like the case with wind power, the

hard part is harnessing that energy and converting it into a form we can use to power hospitals and schools, cars and homes at any hour of the day—or night. To make it both a consistent and a reliable energy source,

Fun Fact:
A 5-time increase in the price of a gumball that originally costs a quarter would raise its price to $1.25. At 50 times more expensive, that gumball would cost $12.50. That's an expensive gumball. How many would you buy?

solar energy must be stored, available at a moment's notice, and converted into a useful form.

We already know how to capture and convert the sun's energy using solar panels. One of the cool things about solar power is that it causes no pollution, except for the panel production process itself! But if solar power's so great, why don't we use more?

Well, for one thing, the cost of solar-generated electricity is between five and fifty times more than fossil fuels (DOI 2005, ix). Those costs are pretty powerful too and are preventing widespread use of solar energy. Until its price is competitive with fossil fuels, there will be little demand for it. The market has spoken!

Solar power may be the energy source of the future and it's a rapidly growing industry. Until technological advances lower prices so that it can compete with existing energy sources like oil and gas, most people will not be willing to pay more for solar power when they can buy fossil fuels for a lot less—even if the government subsidizes it.

Bring the price down and the reliability up, though, and you'll have people lining up around the block to use solar power!

Nuke It!

Nuclear power produces energy by splitting atoms of uranium in a nuclear reactor. When split, the atom fragments release huge amounts of energy that can be used to make electricity.

Once built, nuclear power plants do not emit carbon dioxide. But no new nuclear plants have opened in the United States since 1997, mostly because of safety concerns and high building costs.

Fun Fact:
Alternative energy is any energy source different from what we traditionally, or typically, use. Fossil fuels like oil, gas, and coal are traditional energy sources. They are also called non-renewable because nature will not replenish them in a human life span. Renewable energy sources are those that nature replenishes, such as sun, wind, and water.

Yes, it's true that if not carefully controlled, nuclear radiation can sicken or even kill humans and animals. But here's a technology that has come a long way in the last decade. We know more now than ever before

about managing nuclear energy safely, if only because other countries in Europe and Asia (especially India, China, Japan, and France), have continued to develop such plants.

Of course, accidents and problems still

occur. Technology must be improved in order to make nuclear plants as safe as possible and manage waste in an efficient way.

That said, nuclear energy could be a good solution to our power needs. Nuclear power could become the inexpensive energy source of the near future.

We don't know for sure if the earth's current warming trend is truly a threat. What we *do* know is that using the earth's resources wisely is the right thing to do.

The way to solve the big problems that face the world today is not by going back to the unpleasant lifestyles of centuries ago that both great inventors and average people have worked so hard to change. Rather, it's through the kinds of big ideas innovators and inventors bring to market every day.

That's why people power is the most important power source of all.

How to Become
an Enviropreneur

We've seen that the earth's temperatures
change over time and that the climate has
warmed and cooled many times over our planet's long history. We don't know *how* humans
are involved with this change, or even *if* they
are involved with it.

However, we do know that we live on a
beautiful planet, and we want to keep it that
way! Education, innovation, and a willingness
to adapt to changing conditions with confidence and enthusiasm instead of fear can help
us solve the problems that get in the way.

There's a cool name for the many inno-

Fun Fact:
An entrepreneur is someone who takes the opportunity and the risk of starting a business.

vative people out there who are helping us adapt to a changing world while caring for the environment: "enviropreneurs." Enviropreneurs are entrepreneurs who work for the environment. Enviropreneurs don't force their beliefs on others.

They don't panic about environmental problems. They don't think the government or some other person should fix everything for them. Instead, enviropreneurs look at environmental problems like global warming as opportunities and find ways to fix them. They don't regulate—they innovate!

And this is where the best ideas and inventions come from.

How do enviropreneurs learn to create and innovate? How do they come up with so many good ideas? Enviropreneurs study the world around them.

Enviropreneurs look carefully at the facts. They get information from the market. They look at what people want, buy, and are willing to pay for. Enviropreneurs learn to think for themselves—they don't just automatically believe what someone else says. This is called "critical thinking."

Can kids like you learn how to do all this? Absolutely! In this chapter, we'll show you how to think like an enviropreneur.

Just like you need to exercise your body to make your muscles stronger, you need to exercise your mind so you can make your thinking skills better.

Exercise 1
Understanding How the Market Works

How many people does it take to make a pencil?

Take a look at a wooden pencil. What do you see? Wood, a little paint, lead, a bit of metal to hold the eraser.

Simple…or is it? Let's see!

Take a guess…how many people do you think it takes to make a pencil?

A pencil is made up of wood, some paint to make the wood a pretty color, the lead you write with, the metal to hold the eraser, and the eraser itself. Someone has to make each one of these parts.

Do you think one person makes the whole pencil? Or do you think one person cuts the wood, while a second person makes the eraser, and a third person makes the lead? How many people do you think it takes to make a pencil? One? Five? Ten?

Now, think about all of the people who don't exactly *make* the pencil, but who help the people who do.

For example, the person who paints the pencil probably doesn't make the paint. The painter needs to buy paint from someone who knows how to make paint. Think about all of the people like the paint maker who might *indirectly* help to make the parts of a pencil. What's your guess now? Twenty? Thirty? Fifty?

Even the person who makes the paint needs help! There are lots of chemicals and other things needed to make the paint just the right color.

So the paint maker goes to a chemist to get the chemicals needed to make the paint. When you add people like the chemist, how many people would you guess now? One hundred? Two hundred? Three hundred?

Actually, if we were to really track all the people who are involved with making a pencil, especially those indirectly involved, our list could almost go on forever. Let's take a closer look at exactly how a pencil is made and I think you will get the idea.

The Life Story of a Pencil

A famous essay called "I, Pencil" (Read 1958) shows what has to happen in order to produce a pencil. *Millions* of pencils are made every year by *thousands* of workers!

Although a pencil seems like a simple thing, a lot of work goes into making one. Just how do pencils get made and sent to the people who need to use them? It's through the magic of markets!

First, loggers go into the forest to cut down trees. They use saws and other equipment that someone else makes. Cooks and farmers provide loggers with the food they eat. Construction workers and architects build the places where the loggers live. There are people in charge of running the logging company, taking care of the money the company earns, and building and fixing the trucks and ships that carry the loggers and their logs.

Next, the logs are shipped to a mill where they are cut into smaller pieces of wood. Someone had to make the trucks, boats, and trains to ship the logs. All of these loggers and truck drivers and mill workers have to talk to each other, so someone *else* invented telephones, telephone wires, computer cables, and computers. Although none of these people are *directly* involved in making your pencil, they're all helping in some way.

The mill owner has to keep the mill up and running, so someone has to provide energy and power so the mill can work properly. Once the wood is cut at the mill, it is painted. Someone has to paint the wood, and…you get it, someone has to make the paint, too.

Then, the wood has to be shipped to factories, where the pencils are made. At the factories, there are lots of machines that an engineer had to build. The factory workers put the lead that you write with inside the wood, which is finally cut into the right shape for pencils.

Whew! We've only begun to describe the process to make the wood part of the pencil, and already *hundreds* of people have worked on it directly or indirectly! And the lead, metal, and eraser parts of the pencil are even more complicated.

As you may have guessed, no one person makes a pencil and no one person is dictating what each person must do. Instead, the loggers, the workers at the mills, the workers at the factories, and the people who make the eraser, the metal, and the lead all do just one small part of the work. Together they get it all done, even if they've never met or talked with each other. And *you* end up with a pencil to write with. Pretty cool, huh?

Why do all of these people work so hard at jobs like making erasers that might not seem very important? Because if they do the little part that they know how to do, they can earn money to buy food and houses and everything else they need to live.

The workers have a reason to keep showing up for work and to do a good job. They have an incentive. If they don't show up and work hard, they could lose their jobs. People respond to incentives. And when left to make their own choices, they can produce a lot.

You may have heard of the old Soviet Union. There, the government tried to control the people and factories that make products like pencils. Government agencies determined what was going to be produced, how it was going to be produced, and what price was going to be charged. Government owned the resources necessary for production instead of individual people. This didn't work very well, though, because the government was in control of everything. This meant the government didn't have to worry about doing a good job—no one could fire the government for doing a bad job. The government also didn't have to worry about making good products that people actually wanted to buy.

The government could make whatever it wanted, poorly, and charge what it wanted. The government didn't have all the information that the market provides, such as what people want and how much they are willing to pay for it. The market wasn't allowed to work very well.

This is why markets are so cool. In a free market that's not controlled by government, buyers tell sellers which items they want

Fun Fact:
We take better care of things when we own them as individuals than when we don't. Compare the playground ball, for example, that is left out overnight or kicked on the roof to the one you bought at the store.

simply by buying them. The sellers get the message and make those items available for sale. Sellers tell buyers the cost of the item by the price they charge. If the price of the item is too high, buyers won't buy it and sellers will have to do something different to earn money.

We are lucky in America. We don't rely on the government to do everything for us. We don't rely on the government to tell us how many trees to cut and plant. We don't rely on the government to regulate the amount of gas we use or the quantity of coal we burn.

Instead, "we the people" choose. We choose what to make and how to spend our money. We choose what jobs we'll do to earn that money.

In the end, some people will choose to make a small part of your pencil; others will choose to create new products.

Government can help keep markets working smoothly, mostly by protecting the rights and freedom of citizens to buy and to sell the products they want.

Exercise 2
It's Your Turn—Now You Own the Store!

So we've seen how markets work and we've thought about how many people it can take to make a product. We've also thought about ways to spend your limited amount of money wisely. But what if you were the one *selling* the product instead of *buying* it? What would you do then?

Markets force buyers and sellers to be creative and to come up with new ideas. The move from wood to coal and coal to oil and gas happened because people expected to make money from their new ideas. By creating something newer, better, or cheaper you can earn a profit too. Profit is the money you have left over after you pay what it costs to make and sell something—money that you can take home and spend as you wish.

But making a profit isn't easy. You need a product that people want that you can afford to produce and sell at a price people are willing to pay. That can be tricky.

Here's an example. Have you ever set up a lemonade stand to make some extra money so you could buy something you want? If you made $10 for selling lemonade, but had to spend $5 on lemons, sugar, and ice to make

Fun Fact:
The choice to buy one thing is a choice not to buy something else with that money.

the lemonade, your profit and earnings for time spent would be $5 (the $10 you earned minus the $5 you spent to make the lemonade).

Now, what would you do if you were selling lemonade, but the kid next door opened his own lemonade stand and charged a quarter less per cup? What would you, as a good entrepreneur choose to do?

> A. You could watch him sell lemonade while you sell none.
> B. You could match his price or join him and not compete.
> C. You could lower your price below his so that neighbors would buy from you instead.
> D. You could invent new flavors to make your product better (mango lemonade, anyone?), so people are willing to pay more for your fancy lemonade.
> E. You could shut down your stand and do something else.

Today's energy producers face the same set of choices. They know that people want clean energy, but they also know people aren't willing to pay much more than they're paying now for fossil fuel-based energy. This means there is a huge opportunity right now for anyone who can invent or perfect an alternative energy source. Just think if *you* came up with a clean energy source that could compete with fossil fuels on price, reliability, and convenience; you'd be doing something really meaningful and wonderful—and be rewarded for your efforts with a nice tidy profit!

New technologies bring progress. They are the result of the market process which improves the health and well-being of people worldwide. The creation of new technologies, motivated by the desire for profit has made the world wealthier and healthier.

Our environment is cleaner than ever before, not because the government forces us to make it so, but because companies and individuals are choosing to make it so.

Because we have the leisure time that conveniences provide us, we have the leisure time to think about things like the environment.

Exercise 3
Global Warming and Missed Opportunity

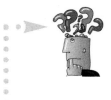

This or That?
Imagine you get $100 for your birthday. How would you spend it?

To get you started, let's look at some popular things you might like to buy. As we've seen, the price of most items in the United States is determined by what sellers are willing to sell it for and what buyers are willing to pay for it. Let's look at some pretend prices and think about what you would choose to spend your money on.

Candy bar - $2.00
Video game console - $35.00
New video game - $30.00
Music downloads - $1.00 per song
Ipod - $80.00
Books for school - $20.00
Donation to a charity - $5.00
A new bike - $50.00
New sneakers - $20.00
Energy efficient light bulbs
    for your room - $10.00
Cell phone - $15.00
Savings account - $10.00
Trip to the mall - $10.00
Dentist visit - $80.00
Computer - $100.00
Dog toys - $3.00

Have you picked out the things you'd like to buy and thought about why you chose those things?

To Buy or Not to Buy?

You probably want more things on this list than you can afford to buy. After all, you only have $100. There are lots of ways to spend the money, of course, but you can only spend it once.

You will have to make a choice. If you buy the bike, a new video game, and some cheap sneakers, that takes all of your $100. You can't buy your dog new toys or download new tunes until you get some more money.

The cost of choosing some items is giving up other ways of spending your money. Buying video games is a *lot* more fun than going to the dentist! But if you have a cavity, you're going to need to go the dentist! And getting that tooth fixed now could be a lot cheaper than doing it later, not to mention the things you won't be able to do with your friends because your tooth hurts. So maybe buying the video game wasn't the best choice in the end because you missed out on other things that are more important to you.

It works exactly the same way for people around the world, and governments too. If you spend money on one thing, you won't have that money to spend on something else. Just like when you spend your $100 birthday money, you have to choose.

In 2004 a group of world-famous economists was asked to make the same kinds of choices. Economists are people who think about how other people choose to use resources, like money.

These economists were given a fake $50 billion to pretend with—not just $100—but the idea was the same. They were asked to choose which ways of spending the money would do the most good for the most people.

The economists divided their possible choices into groups according to what they could buy with each dollar spent. Bad choices were those where a dollar spent provided less than a dollar's worth of benefits. They then listed them in order of priority with what they considered to be the best choices first (Lomborg 2004, 606).

Here is their list of the best and worst ways to solve challenges like disease, malnutrition, lack of clean drinking water, and poverty:

Fun Fact:
Bjorn Lomborg, architect of the study summarized by the table on page 91, was once an active member of Greenpeace. His earth-shaking book, *The Skeptical Environmentalist,* shook even his own ideas at the time. His summary: We live in a better, cleaner, healthier world than ever in history.

This list shows how the economists chose to spend the money in order of importance. And guess what—trying to "fix" global warming, or climate change, landed at the *bottom* of the list! That's because, in just the same way as you must choose how to spend your birthday money, countries only have so much money to spend on things. Even wealthy countries can't afford to do everything.

We need to choose.

Many people are in a frenzy over global warming. They believe government can solve the problem if we just hand over more power and money. But as we've seen, global warming is likely a natural thing that humans don't do very much to cause. It probably can't be stopped even with all the money in the world!

And if it can't be stopped with all that money, why not instead do the things that we know are going to help people adapt to change? Why not do things that help make people healthier and more productive?

If we're going to find a way to "solve" global warming or any other environmental problem, the answer will come from people who have enough time, energy, money, and freedom to use their creativity to solve the problem. It will *not* come from some government agency funded with lots of tax dollars.

RANK		CHALLENGE	OPPORTUNIY
Very Good Opportunities	1	Disease	Control of HIV/AIDS
	2	Malnutrition	Providing micro nutrients
	3	Subsidies and Trade	Trade liberalization
	4	Disease	Control of malaria
Good Opportunities	5	Malnutrition	Development of new agricultural technologies
	6	Sanitation & Water	Small-scale water technology for livelihoods
	7	Sanitation & Water	Community-managed water supply and sanitation
	8	Sanitation & Water	Research on water productivity in food production
	9	Government	Lowering the cost of starting a new business
Fair Opportunities	10	Migration	Lowering barriers to migration for skilled workers
	11	Malnutrition	Improving infant and child nutrition
	12	Malnutrition	Reducing the prevalence of low birth weight
	13	Diseases	Scaled-up basic health services
Bad Opportunities	14	Migration	Guest worker programs for the unskilled
	15	Climate	Optimal carbon tax ($25-$300)
	16	Climate	Kyoto Protocol
	17	Climate	Value-at-risk carbon tax ($100-$450)

Exercise 4
Reducing Our Carbon Footprints

One idea that has gotten a lot of attention recently is the idea of people reducing their "carbon footprints." What does this mean? Your "carbon footprint" is the amount of carbon dioxide you send into the atmosphere. The average footprint for Americans is nineteen metric tons of carbon dioxide per year. In contrast, the average carbon footprint in Kenya is .27 metric ton.

Can you think of ways to make your carbon footprint smaller?

There are all sorts of ways if you put your mind to it. You could use more efficient light bulbs, or you could spend less time on the computer. You could dry your clothes on a clothesline instead of in the dryer and take fewer or shorter showers. You could choose to ride your bike to school instead of taking the bus. All of these changes to your daily activities would shrink your carbon footprint.

But if reducing our carbon footprints is this easy, and Americans have bigger footprints than people in other countries, why don't we just require everyone to shrink their carbon footprint?

First, it is important to remember that

all these changes have consequences.

For instance, while riding a bike saves energy and is a great exercise, it gives you less time to do other things, like sports or home-work. While *you* might be "ok" with these consequences, others may not be.

Second, the difference between the U.S. and other countries' average carbon footprints can be looked at in another way. The United States is the most productive country on Earth!

The average Kenyan doesn't produce much and they can't afford to consume much either. The average household income in Kenya is $1.00 a day. That's probably less than you spend on lunch at school!

In Kenya fewer than one of three houses have running water or a bicycle. The majority of houses have dirt floors, only one in sixteen are connected to the electricity grid, and one of four have a refrigerator. They have a small footprint because they don't use much energy. How would you rather live?

When you send carbon dioxide into the atmosphere, it's because you're using energy. Things like using an air conditioner, driving a car, or running a factory all use energy and create pollution.

That's the price we pay for progress. We drive our car because it gets us to work and play faster.

We sit in an air-conditioned room because it is more comfortable and it enables us to think better and to be more creative. The ideas we come up with may be just the ones needed to solve a big environmental problem!

Fun Fact:
Carbon intensity is the amount of carbon emitted per productive output. It has been declining in the United States for decades. As we make more, we emit less per unit!

Exercise 5
The Cost of Zero Pollution

Imagine a world with no pollution.

Perhaps you've heard that it would be worth spending lots of money to fight global warming because it would be nicer to live in a world with no pollution. Pollution, after all, is the unwanted by-product of human actions

Think about what a world without waste would look like.

- How would you get from place to place?
- What kind of work would there be so that people could feed their families?
- What would your neighborhood look like?
- What kinds of things would you do for fun?
- What would happen if you broke your leg? Who would help you and how?

Fun Fact:
The electricity grid is like a maze that carries electricity from the power source, usually called an electric utility, to your neighborhood and then your house.

Have you thought about it? Once you do, you'll realize the tradeoffs.

Life Without Pollution
What would a world without waste look like? It would look like a world with no production:

no cars, no computers, no video games, no cell phones, no bicycles, no back packs, no books, no campfires, and no freedom to move or do or create.

There would be no electricity, and so none of the things that electricity powers—including all the miracle machines in modern hospitals that save people's lives. There would be nothing to power tractor engines, and so no food other than that which is grown by hand.

All of the things that cause pollution either directly in their use or indirectly in the production of them wouldn't exist.

In fact, if carbon dioxide is considered a pollutant then *breathing* is polluting! Remember, you exhale carbon dioxide with every breath. Claiming that all carbon dioxide is a pollutant is just plain silly. We know that carbon dioxide has a natural cycle and is a vital part of life on Earth. Yet it is also an undesired side-effect of production.

So it's easy to see why there is some amount of pollution that we must accept as a tradeoff for a more comfortable, productive way of life. Some may say that we produce too much "stuff." But isn't that better than producing nothing at all, and living like people did hundreds of years ago—in the dark, without travel or medicine?

The bright side to pollution is the benefits from production; better products and health care, improved travel and communication, more leisure time and greater wealth that allows more people to care more about the environment. The ability to protect the environment comes through freedom— freedom to choose how we live our lives.

Maybe you'll decide to walk or ride your bike to school, saving some fossil fuel energy while you're exerting your own. Or, you may want to ride the bus to school in order to have more time for homework and friends. You're free to choose! And as long as you understand the consequences of what you are doing, the decision you make is likely to be the best one for you.

Of course, your parents and other adults have advice to offer you on what choices to make, and it's smart to listen to them. They are trying to help you make the right decisions and provide you with more information. But only *you* can measure the costs and benefits *you* receive from your actions. Only you know the value you receive by doing one thing instead of another. No one else knows what you want!

It's only human to try to improve our lives. We all want to be happier, healthier, and

Fun Fact:
Stone tools were widely used as much as 2 million years ago. Between 500,000 and 1 million years ago Homo erectus tamed fire. Fire emits carbon dioxide.

97

Fun Fact:
It is also true that you don't know how other people value things or how to decide what is best for them.

more comfortable, and why not? Our lives are better when they are productive, and pollution is a price we pay for that.

There's absolutely nothing wrong with wanting to cut down on pollution, but it shouldn't be at a cost greater than its value. It's only through innovation that we'll find ways to generate more power in ways that pollute less!

Exercise 6
The Big Picture

There is so much information available to us that sometimes it is hard to determine what information is good and what is "garbage." Given that we live in an ever-changing world, what we once thought was good information may soon become garbage. Science helps us move through this learning process.

Like enviropreneurs, we must learn to be critical thinkers. When information is provided, we need to decide if it shows the whole picture or only a part of it. We need to think about whether the picture shows cause and effect, or just a relationship.

We need to evaluate if the picture describes what's really happening. Critical thinking gives you a better understanding of the world. Don't just take what people say as truth; think about it and ask questions. Exploration is the best way to learn.

The following pages tell a story with pictures. They tell a story about climate change. Put on your best critical thinking cap and see if you can figure out the *rest* of the story.

The Hockey Stick

Figures 7 & 8 below show the temperature of the earth over a long period of time. Figure 7 shows the last 100,000 years and figure 8, known as the hockey stick due to its shape, shows the last 1,000 years.

These figures suggest that the earth is warming faster and more than ever before. The information shown in these graphs is one big reason why so many people are freaking out about global warming. Since humans have increased their output of carbon dioxide during this same time period, some people conclude that humans *must* have caused this

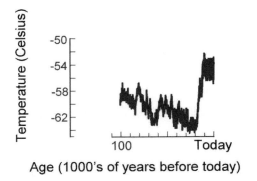

Figure 7: Global temperature estimates, ice core data. *Figure courtesy of Climate and Environmental Physics, University of Bern, Switzerland.*

incredible warming. They say we must act *now* to prevent further warming.

What do you think about these graphs? What can you tell about climate change and the human impact from these pictures?

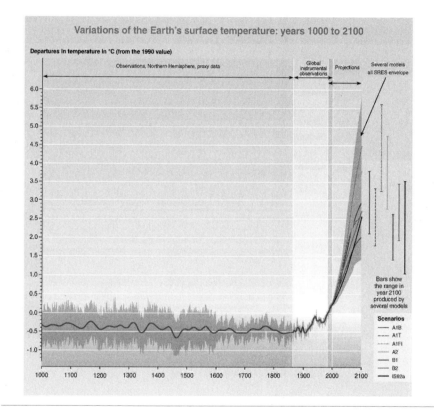

Figure 8: Global temperature estimates, the hockey stick. *Figure courtesy of Climate Change 2001: Synthesis Report, Intergovernmental Panel on Climate Change.*

The Rest of the Story

It is easy to show people information that tells a false story. For example, compare figure 9 to figure 7 on the previous page. When using data as supporting evidence, we must be careful to look at the whole picture.

When we shorten the graph to 100,000 years, as illustrated in figure 7, instead of 650,000 years, as illustrated in figure 9, it appears as though earth temperatures skyrocket like never before.

The *whole* picture, though, shows that the earth has warmed and cooled many times in its long history, way before humans lived on Earth. Neither picture shows conclusive evidence that human action has caused

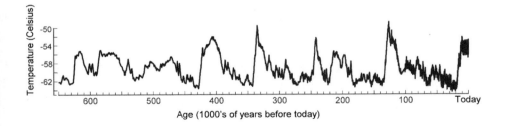

Figure 9: Estimated temperature in Antarctica. *Figure courtesy of Climate and Environmental Physics, University of Bern, Switzerland.*

global warming!

The hockey stick figure was developed using computer modeling. Remember "garbage in, garbage out?" The mathematical accuracy in this computer model has been questioned (see McIntyre and McKintrick 2005a and b and Muller 2004). Nevertheless, it was used by the IPCC in its 2001 summary report.

If you recall, the IPCC is the group of international scientists that are studying climate change. The conclusion drawn by the IPCC was that global temperatures have risen at "rates very likely without precedent during the last 10,000 years," (IPCC 2001, 31). This caused concern, even hysteria, around the globe.

Yet research has found plenty of errors in

the hockey stick model that the IPCC used to draw its conclusions. It should have shown results more like those on the previous page with warming and cooling trends. But we all know that it is sometimes hard to change the mindset of people once they believe something. No one believes the sun revolves around the earth any longer, but it took years to convince people that this was true.

Many people who are afraid of global warming simply haven't seen the whole picture. They have looked at graphs like the one that cut off part of Earth's history. These graphs make today's warming trends look worse than they really are!

When you look at all of history instead of only the last 100,000 years, you realize that today's warming may be part of a warming and cooling cycle that has repeated many times throughout the earth's history. Part of critical thinking is making sure that you have all the facts you can gather and as complete a picture as possible.

Storm Watch

What about all the hype that storms are getting bigger and stronger? Figure 10 shows the total number of hurricanes from all around the world from the years 1970 to 2004. The different lines relate to the different categories of hurricanes measured by wind speed.

The black line is the number of category 1 hurricanes. Category 1 hurricanes are the least powerful with wind speeds between 74 and 95 miles per hour. That is about how fast people drive on the interstate in Montana! The

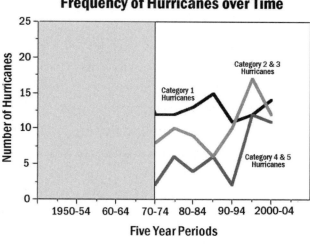

Figure 10: Number of hurricanes and their wind speeds since 1970. *Figure courtesy of P. Webster, et.al [Reprinted with permission of AAAS.]*

lightest grey line is category 2 and 3 hurricanes that carry wind speeds varying from 96 to 130 miles per hour.

The medium grey line is the sum of category 4 and 5 hurricanes, like Katrina in 2005, with wind speeds greater than 131 miles per hour.

Does this diagram lead you to believe that we now have more or fewer hurricanes? There are certainly people who have looked at this picture and decided that both the number of hurricanes and their intensity has increased. They claim this is because of global warming. Are the hurricanes we see today getting stronger, weaker, or staying about the same? Look closely at the picture and think about what you see.

The Rest of the Story

The first picture implied that the number of hurricanes and their intensity has increased over time.

Global warming strikes again! But the facts strike back!

The graph here extends the same data back into the 1950s.

Again, looking at the data over a longer

period of time shows a very different story.
Now it's not so clear that hurricanes are greater
in number or intensity than in the past, is it?

In addition, we have much better technology today to find hurricanes over the
oceans, which we might have missed before, so
of course we should expect more hurricanes to
be discovered today than in the past.

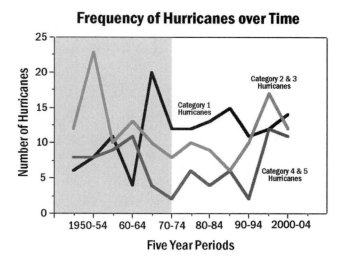

Figure 11: Number of hurricanes since 1950. *Figure courtesy of Chip Knappenberger,
Tech Central Station.*

The Big Meltdown

Many people fear that glaciers are melting as a result of global warming. But is it true?

Well, yes—and no!

While some ice masses are shrinking, others are growing. Let's look at the evidence and see what is really happening here.

Figure 12: The glaciers of Kilimanjaro. *1912 photograph courtesy of Oeler (Public domain); 1970 photo courtesy of Bruno Messerli; 2000 photo courtesy of Lonnie Thompson.*

Mt. Kilimanjaro is a very famous mountain in an African country called Tanzania. Look at the pictures of Mount Kilimanjaro and see if you can solve this puzzle: Why are the glaciers on the mountain getting smaller?

The Rest of the Story

Though many people would like you to believe that the glaciers on Mount Kilimanjaro are melting because of global warming, science tells us there are other factors involved.

The temperatures on the mountain show no warming trend and in fact do not rise above the freezing level (Molg et al. 2003).

Yet the glaciers have been shrinking since about 1880, before any rapid increase in carbon dioxide.

What has changed is the air humidity—it has gone down. The cloud cover has also declined. As a result the ice is evaporating and there is not enough snowfall to replace it (Kaser et al. 2004).

Sometimes we need to question even what seems obvious!

Figure 13: Polar bears on ice.
Photo courtesy of Amanda Byrd.

111

Polar bears adrift

It is said that a picture paints a thousand words. This famous picture of polar bears has been seen around the world. Look closely and think about what words you might choose to describe this photograph.

What does the photo seem to tell us about global warming? Does it say anything about polar bear habitat? How would you interpret it?

The Rest of the Story

This picture of a mama bear and her cub made headlines worldwide. Some said things like, "Global warming sees polar bears stranded on melting ice" and claimed that the bears have become a symbol of global warming. They are a symbol, but is it an accurate and fair symbol?

Not really, because pictures, like pictures sometimes do, can fool the world. The original caption the photographer wrote was *"Mother polar bear and cub on interesting ice sculpture carved by waves"* (WHOI 2004). That's very different from claiming that global warming is stranding polar bears at sea!

The photo was taken on a scientific expedition in 2004. On the day it was taken, a scientist wrote in the ship's journal that:

"A polar bear was sighted swim-
ming off of the ship's port bow. It
looked to be a juvenile [a young
bear] but is still considered to be
very dangerous. Later on a mother
and cub were also spotted on top
of an extraordinary ice block"
(WHOI 2004).

Now read that again. Do you see *anything*
that says that the bears were stranded, or in
distress, or stuck on the iceberg? Polar bears
have been known to swim up to 100 miles. As
for the expedition itself, it was delayed for several days due to heavy ice in the Northwest
Passage, an arctic waterway!

What Would You Say to Chicken Little?

When Chicken Little thought that the acorn tucked into her feathers was actually a piece of falling sky, she scared herself and all of her friends. Once she saw the acorn and realized what had happened, she stopped being scared.

Global warming is like that. Now that you understand that it is probably a natural part of the earth's evolution, something humans have seen before and will see again, doesn't it make you less worried?

The best way to help conserve resources, to help animals, and to keep wild places wild, is to make responsible choices for yourself based on the facts.

Knowledge really *is* power. And in the case of global warming, there are plenty of facts available. Some point towards danger ahead, others don't. There's so much more we need to know.

Searching for the truth about our incredible world, discovering new facts and new technologies, and using them to make smarter choices is what science is all about.

Science is a continual learning process. Never let anyone tell you that "the case is closed" when it comes to global warming, weather, and climate.

There are so many mysteries yet to solve on our way to a healthier, happier and cleaner world…and human ingenuity and innovation will help get us there.

So become an enviropreneur. Learn all you can about our amazing planet and the people that live on it. Learn how to think for yourself. Look at the big picture before deciding what you believe and keep an open mind. That way, you'll be ready to create the new products and ideas that will help all of us and the planet, too.

What is the best and most important resource in the world? *You are!* Think about that for a minute. There are 6.5 billion people on the planet, and not one of them is exactly like you. Every time you think about something, you're doing it in a way that no one else does…and that's the way problems big and small get solved.

When you really think about it, people aren't the problem when it comes to a changing climate—they are the solution! Human innovation and creativity have already changed the world for the better countless times…and they will again.

And that's why it's OK to chill about global warming!

A Word to Parents

This book is the product of concern and love of the environment and the world that we live in. As a mom and an optimist, I envision a future that is wealthier and healthier for all. To ensure such progress, however, we must teach our children to be critical thinkers.

Not critical in the sense of being negative and fearful; rather, critical in the sense of carefully evaluating the world around them, questioning what they see, and valuing education as a means to getting answers.

I wrote this book with a desire to show readers, young and old, the connection between our freedoms and environmental quality. It is those freedoms that allow us to choose the methods that are most appropriate to protecting the environment. It is those freedoms that allow us to explore the unknown and use our creativity and ingenuity to solve problems.

I am grateful to the many scientists, economists, teachers, principals, editors, and friends who reviewed this book for accuracy.

Of course, any errors and omissions remain my own. To keep the book readable for a younger audience, some technical ideas have been simplified but great effort has been taken to maintain factual accuracy and integrity. It's also for this reason that I've included citations and a full bibliography, for readers wanting to learn more about this important and fascinating topic.

Take a look, read through the pages, and decide for yourself.

How do you choose to live your life and how can we together make this world a better place for all children of the future?

Thank Yous

I'd like to extend my gratitude to all those who helped me create this book. Great thanks goes to the scientists and other reviewers and editors for keeping me on track:

Dr. Timothy Ball, Environmental Consultant, former professor of climatology at the University of Winnipeg, Chairman of the Natural Resources Stewardship Project;

Dr. David Evans, founder of Science Speak and a developer of FullCAM, a leading carbon accounting model that estimates carbon in plants, debris, mulch, soils, and forestry, and agricultural products;

Michael R. Fox, Director, Center for Science, Climate, and the Environment, Grassroot Institute of Hawaii;

Dr. Richard Lindzen, Alfred P. Sloan Professor of Atmospheric Sciences, MIT;

George Taylor, Certified Consulting Meteorologist;

and Marc Morano, Communications Director, Senate Environment and Public Works Committee.

I appreciate the comments and assistance from fellow PERCies and associates, mentors, and friends, including:

Terry Anderson, Director, the Property and Environment Research Center (PERC), Senior Fellow at the Hoover Institution, and an adjunct professor at the Stanford Graduate School of Business;

Tim Fitzgerald, PhD Student, resource economics at the University of Maryland, cowboy, guide, and outfitter;

Peter J. Hill, George F. Bennett Professor of Economics at Wheaton College of Wheaton, Illinois, and a Senior Fellow of the Property and Environment Research Center (PERC);

and Brandon Scarborough, Research Fellow, the Property and Environment Research Center (PERC), and my personal science consultant.

I thank my parents, Bruce and Barbara Lippke, for always motivating me to push beyond the box.

And of course, the greatest gratitude goes to my family—Colter, Jake, and Mike—who put up with my bizarre hours, help me brainstorm new and creative ideas, and encourage me to be an enviropreneur. I love you guys!

References

Benitez, L.E. et al. 2007. The economics of windpower with energy storage. *Energy Economics.* DOI: 10.1016/ j.eneco.2007.01.017.

Caldeira, Ken and A.K. Jain. 2003. Climate sensitivity uncertainty and the need for energy without CO2 emissions. *Science.* 299: 2052–2054. DOI: 10.1126/ science.1078938.

Carter, Robert M., C.R. de Freitas, Indur M. Goklany, David Holland, and Richard S. Lindzen. 2006. The Stern Review: A Dual Critique. *World Economics.* 7(4): 165–232. October –December.

Coon, Charli E., J.D. 2001. Why the Government's CAFE Standards for Fuel Efficiency Should Be Repealed, not Increased. *Heritage Foundation Backgrounder* #1458. July 11.

Davis, R.E., P.C. Knappenberger, P.J. Michaels, M.W. Novikov. 2003. "Changing Heat-Related Mortality in the United States." *Environmental Health Perspectives.* 14: 1712–1718.

Department of Energy. 2005. *Basic Research Needs for Solar Energy Utilization.* Available: http://www.sc.doe.gov/bes/reports/files/ SEU_rpt.pdf (accessed May 23, 2007).

Fischer, Hubertus, Martin Wahlen, Jesse Smith, Derek Mastroianna, and Bruce Deck. 1999. Ice core records of atmospheric carbon dioxide around the last three glacial terminations. *Science.* 283 (5408): 1712–1714.

Foley, Jonathan A. 2005. Tipping Points in the Tundra. *Science.* 310 (5748): 627 – 628. DOI: 10.1126/science.1120104. 28 October.

Goklany, Indur. 2005. Living with Global Warming. *NPCA Policy Report No. 278.* National Center for Policy Analysis. ISBN #1-56808-148-0. Dallas: Texas. September.

Holgate, S.J. 2007. "On the Decadal Rate of Sea Level Change During the Twentieth Century." *Geophysical Research Letters.* I 34: L01602, DOI:10.1029/ 2006GL028492.

IPCC. 2001. Climate Change Synthesis Report. Summary for Policy Makers. Available: http://www.ipcc.ch/pub/un/syreng/spm.pdf (Accessed July 27, 2007).

IPCC. 2007. Climate Change 2007: The Physical Science Basis. Summary for Policy Makers. Available: http://www.ipcc.ch/ SPM2feb07.pdf (Accessed July 13, 2007).

IUCN/SSC Polar Bear Specialist Group. 2005. Proceedings from the 14th Working Meeting of the IUCN/SSC Polar Bear Specialist Group, Seattle, WA, 20 to 24 June. Available: pbsg.npolar.no (Accessed July 27, 2007).

Johannessen, Ola M., Kirill Khvorostovsky, Martin W. Miles, Leonid P. Bobylev. 2005. "Recent Ice-Sheet Growth in the Interior of Greenland." *Science.* 310 (5750):1013 – 1016. DOI: 10.1126/science.1115356. November 11.

Jordan, James, and James Powell. 2007. The False Hope of Biofuels. *Washington Post.* July 2. B07.

Kaser G., D.R. Hardy, T. Molg, R.S. Bradley, and T.M. Hyera. 2004. "Modern Glacial Retreat on Kilimanjaro as Evidence of Climate Change: Observations and Facts." *International Journal of Climatology.* 24: 329-39.

Kilcik, Ali. 2005. Regional sun climate interaction. *Journal of Atmospheric and Solar-Terrestrial Physics.* 67(16):1573–1579, November.

King, David A. 2004. Climate Change Science: Adapt, Mitigate, or Ignore? *Science.* 303: 176–177. January 9.

Lambeck, Kurt and John Chappell. 2001. "Sea Level Change Through the Last Glacial Cycle." *Science.* 292 (5517): 679 – 686.DOI:

10.1126/science.1059549. April 27.

Lomborg, B. (Ed.). 2004. *Global crises, global solutions.* Cambridge, UK/ New York: Cambridge University Press.

Lomborg, B. (Ed.). 2006. *How to spend $50 billion to make the world a better place.* Cambridge, UK /New York: Cambridge University Press.

Lomborg, Bjorn. 2007. Subcommittee on Energy and Environment joint hearing with the Energy and Commerce Committee's Subcommittee on Energy and Air Quality. *Perspectives on Climate Change.* March 21. Available: http://gop.science.house.gov/ hearings/energy07/March%2021/lomborg.pdf

McIntyre, Stephen and Ross McKitrick (2005a) The M&M Critique of the MBH98 Northern Hemisphere Climate Index: Update and Implications *Energy and Environment* 16(1) pp. 69-100.

McIntyre, Stephen and Ross McKitrick (2005b) Hockey Sticks, Principal Components and Spurious Significance *Geophysical Research Letters* Vol. 32, No. 3, L03710 10.1029/2004GL021750 12 February 2005.

Molg, T., Hardy, D.R. and Kaser, G. 2003. Solar-radiation-maintained glacier recession on Kilimanjaro drawn from combined ice-radiation geometry modeling. *Journal of*

Geophysical Research 108: 10.1029/2003JD003546.

Muller, Richard. 2004. "Global Warming Bombshell." *Technology Review.* MIT.

Read, Leonard E. 1958. "I, Pencil: My Family Tree as Told by Leonard E. Read." *The Library of Economics and Liberty.* Available: http://www.econlib.org/LIBRARY/Essays/rdPncl1.html. Accessed July 4, 2007.

Scarborough, Brandon. 2007. "Trading Forest Carbon: The Panacea or Pipe Dream to Address Climate Change." *PERC Policy Series 40.* PERC: Bozeman, MT. July.

Shelton, Jay. 1982. *Jay Shelton's Solid Fuels Encyclopedia.* Garden Way Publishing. Charlotte, VT. December.

Stocker, Thomas. 2007. From polar ice cores to better climate models. *International Pacific Research Center.* 7(1): 13–15.

Thresher, Ronald, J.A. Koslow, A.K. Morison, and D. C. Smith. 2007. Depth-mediated reversal of the effects of climate change on long-term growth rates of exploited marine fish. *Proceedings of the National Academy of Sciences of the United States of America.* Published online before print April 25, 2007. 10.1073/pnas.0610546104.

Vaughan, David. 2005. OCEANS: How Does the Antarctic Ice Sheet Affect Sea Level

Rise? *Science.* 308 (5730): 1877 – 1878. DOI: 10.1126/science.1114670. June 24.

Waghorn, G.C. and S.L. Woodward. 2004. *Ruminant Contributions to Methane and Global Warming—A New Zealand Perspective.* Presented at The Science of Changing Climates—Impact on Agriculture, Forestry and Wetlands. University of Alberta. Edmonton. July 20–23.

Wigley, T.M.L. 1998. The Kyoto Protocol: Carbon dioxide, CH4 and climate implications. *Geophysical Research Letters.* 25(13): 2285–2288. July 1.

Woods Hole Oceanographic Institution (WHOI). 2004. Cruise – 2004 Dispatches. Dispatch 2, August 7-8, 2004, By Kris Newhall. Beaufort Gyre Exploration Project. August. Available: http://www.whoi.edu/ beaufortgyre/dispatch2004/dispatch02.html. Accessed August 2, 2007.